WORKBOOK
& COMPANION to

Bob Proctor's
CHANGE YOUR
**PARADIGM,
CHANGE
YOUR LIFE**

THE ONLY AUTHORIZED
WORKBOOK & COMPANION to

Bob Proctor's

CHANGE YOUR PARADIGM, CHANGE YOUR LIFE

How to Apply the Paradigm Shift to Your Life

Proctor Gallagher Institute

> **Note:** This is the only authorized Workbook and Companion to Bob Proctor's *Change Your Paradigm, Change Your Life*.

Published 2025 by Gildan Media LLC
aka G&D Media
www.GandDmedia.com

CHANGE YOUR PARADIGM, CHANGE YOUR LIFE WORKBOOK. Copyright © 2025 Proctor Gallagher Institute, LP. All rights reserved.

Printed in the United States of America. No part of this book may be used, reproduced or transmitted in any manner whatsoever, by any means (electronic, photocopying, recording, or otherwise), without the prior written permission of the author, except in the case of brief quotations embodied in critical articles and reviews. No liability is assumed with respect to the use of the information contained within. Although every precaution has been taken, the author and publisher assume no liability for errors or omissions. Neither is any liability assumed for damages resulting from the use of the information contained herein.

Front cover design by Patti Knoles

Interior design by Meghan Day Healey of Story Horse, LLC

Library of Congress Cataloging-in-Publication Data is available upon request

ISBN: 978-1-7225-0722-0

10 9 8 7 6 5 4 3 2 1

Contents

Introduction 7

Chapter One 13
Your Awesome Power to Change

Chapter Two 20
Are You Living in Someone Else's Paradigm?

Chapter Three 28
Developing the Confidence to Change Your Paradigm

Chapter Four 36
Paradigms and Cybernetics: *Setting your Control System to Achieve Your Desired Results*

Chapter Five 45
How Your Beliefs Affect Your Paradigm

Chapter Six 56
The Paradigm for Power Performance

Chapter Seven 67
The Lessons of Gratitude in Freedom

Chapter Eight 76
The Benefits of Changing Your Paradigm

Chapter Nine 85
Making Your Positive Paradigm a Habit for Life

Chapter Ten 94
Continuing On

Finally . . . 97

Introduction

You have in your hands a book that can change your life by changing your thinking. It is a workbook for Bob Proctor's *Change Your Paradigm, Change Your Life*. It's not a replacement for that book. It is a workbook that will help you put its dynamic and transformative ideas to work for you. This is the only authorized workbook for *Change Your Paradigm, Change Your Life*.

Paradigm (pronounced *par*-a-dime) is a funny word. You see it crop up in lots of places, but what does it mean?

The word comes from the ancient Greek *paradeigma*, which means *model*. But it has come to have a different meaning today.

In 1962, historian of science Thomas S. Kuhn published an important and influential book called *The Structure of Scientific Revolutions*. He talked about how scientific views of the world have changed over the centuries.

The best-known example comes from 500 years ago. Up to that point, educated people in the Western world believed that the sun and the planets revolved around the earth. But in 1543, a Polish monk named Nicolaus Copernicus published a book that proved the earth and the other planets revolved around the sun.

This discovery created a huge upheaval. In fact Copernicus' model—that is, paradigm—didn't completely catch on for a century. But eventually it did. Astronomers now had to think of a universe that was in many ways the opposite of what they thought it had been. Kuhn called this a *paradigm shift*.

This shift changed the way that our civilization saw the world and our place in it. Some people objected to it, but this sun-centered paradigm—the fact that the sun and not the earth is the center of our solar system—is now universally accepted.

What, you may ask, does all of this have to do with me?

Our society has paradigms that help explain the history of the earth, the cosmos, humanity, and many other things. In addition to these collective paradigms, each of us has our individual paradigms, which are, so to speak, the lenses through which we view the world.

These paradigms vary hugely from person to person. They're basic beliefs about the way the world is—not just about which planet goes around which, but about human life and destiny—including our own.

Your paradigm—the set of ideas that motivate your habits and your day-to-day behavior—will to a great extent dictate how your life goes. It will determine your success, your happiness, your health, even your luck.

Most people live with unconscious paradigms: beliefs about the world that they picked up from parents, teachers, friends, society, and religion. These beliefs were mostly implanted in us from a very young age, when we didn't know we could choose them or not.

Very few people realize that they can change their paradigm. But you can—and that's what Bob Proctor's *Change Your Paradigm, Change Your Life* is all about. This workbook will help you understand, internalize, and implement Bob's ideas. It will transform your life in ways that today you may not even believe possible.

Introduction

At its most basic level, a paradigm is a mental program situated in your subconscious that has almost exclusive control over all your habitual behavior—and almost all of your behavior is habitual.

Paradigms are a multitude of habits passed down from generation to generation, and they manifest themselves in many ways. Paradigms are the way you view yourself, the world, and opportunity. They are how you approach change and challenges. Once you realize that almost all of your behavior is controlled by paradigms, the way you look at the entire world will change.

Bob's book will give you the key to freeing yourself from limiting paradigms and to changing your paradigm—your underlying mental programming—to transform your finances, health, career, relationships, and life.

Bob Proctor is the perfect teacher to take you on this journey. Bob studied the mind and human potential with some of the greatest experts on the subject. In 1961, he started studying the success classic *Think and Grow Rich* by Napoleon Hill, and it transformed his life. Bob listened to recordings by personal development legend Earl Nightingale thousands of times. Bob also worked shoulder to shoulder with Earl Nightingale and his company, the Nightingale-Conant Corporation, from 1968 to 1973, before leaving to start his own personal development company. In 2008, he partnered with Sandy Gallagher to form the Proctor Gallagher Institute. Today millions have been inspired by Bob through the hit movie *The Secret*, his books, including his *New York Times* best seller *You Were Born Rich*, his coaching programs, and live events.

Sadly, Bob is no longer with us. He died in 2022, at the age of eighty-seven. But his ideas and practices are still very much with us, and you can still use them to change your life.

Your Personal Paradigm

In order to shift your personal paradigm, you first have to know what it is. This quiz will give you some idea.

You will see a list of statements below. Rate them in terms of how much you agree with them. If you agree with one very strongly, rate it at 5. If you completely disagree with it, rate it at 1. Rate it at 2, 3, or 4 if you're somewhere in between.

1 Strongly disagree
2 Disagree somewhat
3 Neither agree nor disagree
4 Agree somewhat
5 Strongly agree

____ 1. Life sucks.
____ 2. The odds are stacked against me.
____ 3. It's not what you know, it's *who* you know.
____ 4. I just can't get ahead.
____ 5. It's too late for me to change.
____ 6. Success is for other people, not me.
____ 7. I spend a lot of time feeling sorry for myself.
____ 8. You just can't win.
____ 9. I've been dealt a lousy hand in life.
____ 10. I just don't have any luck.
____ Total

Scoring

Now add up the sum of the numbers you've written down. Here is how to interpret your score.

40–50. You have a pretty negative view of the world and of yourself. These beliefs are very likely standing in the way of getting what you want out of life.

30–40. You are not completely negative, but you tend to look on the downside of things.

20–30. You're slightly inclined toward the positive, but you still have many doubts.

10–20. You have a generally bright outlook on life, but there is probably plenty of room for improvement.

Note that you hear many of these statements frequently from many different sources. They are present everywhere in our culture, like viruses. And as with viruses, you can pick them up whether you know it or not.

But you are not married to any of your beliefs, no matter how strongly you hold them or how far they go back in your life. Bob Proctor's book—with this workbook as an accompaniment—will show you how to change them.

Chapter One

Your Awesome Power to Change

Now go to Bob's book and read the foreword by Sandy Gallagher and chapter 1: "Your Awesome Power to Change." When you have finished, answer the following questions.

Writing is a central focus of this workbook. You can write down the answers to these and other questions in this workbook in the space provided. If you need more space for them, you can get a separate notebook and write down your responses there. In the long run, you will probably want to get a notebook that you will dedicate to this work.

1. How did you feel after reading the chapter? Happy? Sad? Excited? Frustrated?
   _____
   _____

2. What was the single most important idea for you?
   _____
   _____

3. What surprised you the most?
   _____
   _____

4. What did you disagree with or object to?
_____
_____

5. What did you most agree with?
_____
_____

6. What idea excited you the most?
_____
_____

7. What is Bob saying about human potential—yours and everyone else's?
_____
_____

8. Do you believe that what Bob is saying is truly possible for you?
_____
_____

Chapter Review

Write down the three concepts in this chapter that are most important to you. Feel free to do it from memory, or look through the chapter again if you like: after all, you are doing this for yourself.

1. _____
_____
2. _____
_____
3. _____
_____

Inspirational Books

In chapter 1, Bob mentions several books that he found especially helpful and inspirational. Below, write down the titles of ten books that have particularly inspired you. They can be of any type: sacred texts, self-help books, pop philosophy, even children's books.

1. _____
2. _____
3. _____
4. _____
5. _____
6. _____
7. _____
8. _____
9. _____
10. _____

Of these books, choose the one that has been the *most important* to you. Write down why—what you found most inspirational or helpful. Pay particular attention to the mood or feeling you experienced when you read or even think of this book. Then go on to write about how it changed your life. As always, feel free to write as much as you want.

What's Your Paradigm?

Now that you have some idea of what Bob means by a personal paradigm, write down what you believe your own paradigm to be at present. You can write this out in the form of ten statements (space for which follows), or you can write it all out in a single passage—whatever works best for you.

1. _____

2. _____

3. _____

4. _____

5. _____

6. _____

7. _____

8. _____

9. _____

10. _____

Which of these has been the MOST helpful to you in your life?
_____
_____

Which of these has been the LEAST helpful?
_____
_____

The Law of Attraction

In this same chapter, Bob also describes the law of attraction. Write down the definition here, either from your own memory, or, if you need to refresh your memory, go to page 11.

_____
_____
_____

1. How do you understand the law of attraction?
   _____
   _____

2. Does the law of attraction seem plausible to you?
   _____
   _____

3. Have you found any instances of this law working in your life? If so, write down one or two.
   _____
   _____

4. Bob also says that the law of attraction is a secondary law: the primary law is the law of vibration. Again, write down the law from your memory. If you need to remind yourself, look it up on page 11.
   _____
   _____

5. How does the law of attraction relate to the law of vibration?
   _____
   _____

6. List one or two instances of your observations of the law of vibration at work.
   _____
   _____

Chapter Quiz

Now let's go on to see your reactions more specifically. Here are ten statements from chapter 1. Again, rate them in terms of how much you understand and agree with them. If you both understand and agree with a statement very strongly, rate it at 5. If you completely disagree with or don't understand it, rate it at 1. Rate it at 2, 3, or 4 if you're somewhere in between.

    1 Don't understand or strongly disagree
    2 Understand a little but disagree somewhat
    3 Neither agree nor disagree
    4 Mostly understand and agree
    5 Understand well and strongly agree

____ 1. "Success in any undertaking totally depends on what's going on inside our minds; it's got nothing to do with what's going on outside."

____ 2. "If you objectively observe your own behavior for two or three hours from the time you get up in the morning, you'll see that most of your behavioral patterns are not going to give you the success you desire."

____ 3. "Every day, you do the same things, because you're programmed to do them."

____ 4. "You become what you think about."

____ 5. "When you change the way you look at something, what you look at changes."

____ 6. "The law of cause and effect is the law of laws: what you put out comes back."

____ 7. "There's perfection within every one of us, and that perfection seeks to express itself within and through us."

____ 8. "We should never be satisfied with what we've got."

_____ 9. "The magic word is *attitude*."
_____ 10. "We have to create awareness that what we're doing, our habitual behavior, is not producing the results we want."
_____ Total

Scoring

Now add up the sum of the numbers you've written down. Here is how to interpret your score.

10–20. You don't seem to be very sympathetic to the ideas in this chapter or may not understand them.

20–30. You are resistant to these ideas, but not completely.

30–40. You're somewhat open to these ideas.

40–50. You understand and are very receptive to these ideas.

If your score is under 40, you may have some difficulty either understanding or accepting the ideas in this chapter. You may want to reread it. If your score is over 40, you can go on to chapter 2 with confidence.

Compare your score with this quiz with your score from the previous quiz on page 10. What conclusions do you draw? Write out your responses here.

One Final Question

Write out in your own words what a paradigm is.

_____

_____

_____

Chapter Two

Are You Living in Someone Else's Paradigm?

*N*ow go to Bob's book and read chapter 2. Take a moment to check in with yourself. When you have finished, answer the following questions.

1. How did you feel after reading the chapter? Happy? Sad? Excited? Frustrated?
   _____
   _____

2. What was the single most important idea for you?
   _____
   _____

3. What surprised you the most?
   _____
   _____

4. What did you disagree with or object to?
   _____
   _____

5. What did you most agree with?
   _____
   _____

6. What idea excited you the most?
   _____
   _____

7. Comment on this idea: "Almost everyone has had their paradigm built for them—a parent, a guardian, someone else—and it controls their whole lives." Do you agree? Disagree? Use examples from your own life to illustrate your point.
   _____
   _____
   _____

8. Bob discusses a principle called "thinking from the end." Explain this concept in your own words.
   _____
   _____
   _____

Goal Setting

Bob tells us that in order to shape your future, you have to be willing and able to change your paradigm. The first step is to have a purpose in life—a reason for getting out of bed in the morning. Napoleon Hill called it a, "Definite Chief Aim."

What is your central purpose? Write it down below.

If you're not entirely clear about your purpose, write down some thoughts about what it might be (using separate paper if necessary). Once you have done so, condense them into a short, one- or two-sentence statement of your purpose.

If you're not able to complete this process at this point, set it aside and come back to it later.

_____
_____

Now let's be more specific about goals. Write out goals about how you would like to live, where you would like to live, what you would like to do, what you would like to earn, and whom you would like to be with. Write down ten goals, stated in the present tense: that is, don't write, "I will make $250,000 a year." Write "I am making $250,000 a year."

1. _____
2. _____
3. _____
4. _____
5. _____
6. _____
7. _____
8. _____
9. _____
10. _____

Write down these statements three times each morning. Do this practice every day.

On the first day, after completing this exercise, write out a couple of sentences about your mood: how you're feeling, what you're thinking, whether you're excited about your life. Set these aside for a week. Don't look at them in the meantime.

When you have done this practice for a week, again write out a couple of sentences about how you're feeling, what you're thinking, and whether you're excited about your life.

Compare these with the lines you wrote a week before. Do you notice any differences? What do you conclude?

A, B, and C Goals

In this chapter, Bob talks about the difference between A, B, and C goals. Write down your own goals according to this classification. Write down at least three, although you can write as many as you want.

A GOALS

Goals that you already know you can achieve.

1. _____
2. _____
3. _____

B GOALS

Goals that you are fairly sure you can achieve.

1. _____
2. _____
3. _____

C GOALS

Goals that you are far from sure you can achieve; goals that will require a real stretch, those you have no idea of how to attain.

1. _____
2. _____
3. _____

Once you've divided your goals into these categories, consider this statement of Bob's:

"If you hold the picture in your mind and you stay emotionally involved, it will reveal itself. Seek first this kingdom and its expansion in righteousness, and all these things will be given to you. You're going to attract everything that's necessary. If you hold the picture, everything you need will come to you when you need it, but not before."

What are your thoughts and feelings about this passage? Write them down here.

_____
_____
_____
_____

Using the scale of 1 to 5 (1 if you completely disagree, 5 if you completely agree, etc.), rate how much you agree with the following statement:

I am certain of my purpose, and in one way or another, I focus all my energies toward that purpose.   1   2   3   4   5

Now write down three ways of living and working according to your purpose. If you have circled 5 in answer to the question above, write out how you are expressing your purpose in your day-to-day activities. If you have circled a number less than 5, write out possible ways you can achieve your purpose.

1. _____
_____

2. _____
_____

3. _____
_____

Chapter Quiz

Here are ten statements from chapter 2. Again, rate them in terms of how much you understand and agree with them. If you understand and agree with a statement very strongly, rate it at 5. If you completely disagree with or don't understand it at all, rate it at 1. Rate it at 2, 3, or 4 if you're somewhere in between.

1. Don't understand or strongly disagree
2. Disagree or don't understand somewhat
3. Neither agree nor disagree
4. Understand and agree somewhat
5. Understand well and strongly agree

____ 1. "The subconscious mind, which operates according to your paradigm, is wide open, and everything that's going on around goes right into it."

____ 2. "In the absence of clearly defined goals, we become strangely loyal to performing daily trivia until we ultimately become enslaved by them."

____ 3. "Your subconscious mind expresses itself through your actions."

____ 4. "The universal intelligence of the subconscious mind functions in a lawful way, and it works exactly the same way for everyone."

____ 5. "When you impress an idea over and over upon the subconscious, that idea must by law manifest through you."

____ 6. "The paradigm is the picture that controls your behavior and gives you the results you want."

____ 7. "Thinking from the end is the beginning of all miracles."

____ 8. "Any idea that's held in the mind and emphasized, whether feared or revered, will at once begin to clothe itself in the most convenient and appropriate form available."

____ 9. "The future must become the present in the imagination of the one who would wisely and consciously create circumstances."

____ 10. "The ability comes with the desire."

____ Total

Scoring

Now add up the sum of the numbers you've written down. Here is how to interpret your score.

10–20. You don't seem to understand or sympathize much with the ideas in this chapter.

20–30. You have difficulty understanding or are resistant to these ideas, but not completely.

30–40. You understand and are receptive to these ideas to some extent.

40–50. You're very receptive to these ideas.

If your score is under 40, you may have some difficulty either understanding or accepting the ideas in this chapter. You may want to reread it. If your score is over 40, you can go on to chapter 3 with confidence.

Central Points

Write down three points from this chapter that have made the strongest impression on you.

1. _____
   _____
   _____

2. _____
   _____
   _____

3. _____
   _____
   _____

Chapter Three

Developing the Confidence to Change Your Paradigm

Now go to Bob's book and read chapter 3. Take a moment to check in with yourself. When you have finished, answer the following questions. Feel free to write as much as you like—either in the space below or in your notebook.

1. How did you feel after reading the chapter? Happy? Sad? Excited? Frustrated?
   _____
   _____

2. What was the single most important idea for you?
   _____
   _____

3. What surprised you the most?
   _____
   _____

4. What did you disagree with or object to?
   _____
   _____

5. What did you most agree with?
   _____
   _____

6. What idea excited you the most?
   _____
   _____

7. How do you respond to this statement of Bob's: "If you focus your attention on what *you* think of you, everything will work out pretty well?"
   _____
   _____

8. Write down your thoughts about this definition of success: "Success is a progressive realization of a worthy ideal."
   _____
   _____

Doing What You Love

This chapter tells us that you don't go to work for money. You go to work for satisfaction. It has been said that you should do what you love. Write down below five things you love to do, even if and when you're not getting paid for them.

1. _____
2. _____
3. _____
4. _____
5. _____

Once you've done this, look at your list and draw a circle around the single thing you love to do most. Is there a way to make this activity earn money for you? Write down three possible ways.

1. _____
   _____
2. _____
   _____
3. _____
   _____

Who Are You?

In this chapter, we read this quote: "If I want to be free, I've got to be me. Not the me I think you think I should be, not the me I think my wife thinks I should be, not the me I think my kids think I should be. If I want to be free, I've got to be me. I'd better know who me is."

Who are you? What comes to your mind when you are faced with this question? Write out your thoughts below in as much detail as you want. Use "I am" statements.

_____
_____
_____
_____
_____
_____
_____
_____
_____
_____
_____
_____

Your Level of Confidence

The chapter points out that confidence comes from knowledge. Write down below ten tasks that you are confident you can perform. You can relate these to the A and B goals discussed in the previous chapter.

1. _____
2. _____
3. _____
4. _____
5. _____
6. _____
7. _____
8. _____
9. _____
10. _____

Now write down ten things you would love to be able to do but think are out of your reach. You can relate these to the C goals from the previous chapter.

1. _____
2. _____
3. _____
4. _____
5. _____
6. _____
7. _____
8. _____
9. _____
10. _____

Go through the second list and circle the item that you would love to do the most if you could. What would be the best way to get started on it?

_____
_____
_____
_____
_____
_____

What Others Think

This chapter also stresses that we spend a great deal of time and energy worrying about what others think of us. Write down below ten statements that you believe others say about you. Include both positive and negative comments.

1. _____
2. _____
3. _____
4. _____
5. _____
6. _____
7. _____
8. _____
9. _____
10. _____

Now look over your list and draw a circle around the item that gives you the most satisfaction. Then draw a circle around the statement that worries or bothers you the most.

What You Want Others to Think

Now write down statements that you would most like to have others make about you.

1. _____

2. _____

3. _____

4. _____

5. _____

6. _____

7. _____

8. _____

9. _____

10. _____

Look over these statements and circle the one that is most important to you.

Chapter Quiz

Here are ten statements from chapter 3. Again, rate them in terms of how much you understand and agree with them. If you both understand and agree with a statement very strongly, rate it at 5. If you completely disagree with or don't understand it, rate it at 1. Rate it at 2, 3, or 4 if you're somewhere in between.

    1 Don't understand or strongly disagree
    2 Understand a little but disagree somewhat
    3 Neither agree nor disagree
    4 Mostly understand and agree
    5 Understand well and strongly agree

____ 1. "We tend to minimize the things we can do and the goals we can accomplish, and we think other people can accomplish things that we cannot."

____ 2. "What you think of me is none of my business."

____ 3. "If you knew how little other people were thinking, you wouldn't be concerned with what they're thinking."

____ 4. "Anyone could become wealthy."

____ 5. "Success is not where you are, it's where you're going."

____ 6. "Your actions are caused by your paradigm, not by how much you know."

____ 7. "What you think of yourself is very important. What other people think of you is not important."

____ 8. "You can become wealthy by having several sources of income."

____ 9. "If you're not interested in making money, it's because your paradigm is trying to stop you."

____ 10. "If you're working toward a predetermined goal, you're creating; you're doing what God meant for you to do."

____ Total

Scoring

Now add up the sum of the numbers you've written down. Here is how to interpret your score.

10–20. You don't seem to be very sympathetic to the ideas in this chapter or may not understand them.

20–30. You are resistant to these ideas, but not completely.

30–40. You're somewhat open to these ideas.

40–50. You understand and are very receptive to these ideas.

If your score is under 40, you may have some difficulty either understanding or accepting the ideas in this chapter. You may want to reread it. If your score is over 40, you can go on to chapter 4 with confidence.

Central Points

Now write down three points in this chapter that are most important for you.

1. _____

2. _____

3. _____

Chapter Four

Paradigms and Cybernetics

Setting Your Control System to Achieve Your Desired Results

Go to Bob's book and read chapter 4. Take a moment to check in with yourself. When you have finished, answer the following questions. Feel free to write as much as you like—either in the space below or in your notebook.

1. How did you feel after reading the chapter? Happy? Sad? Excited? Frustrated?
   _____
   _____

2. What was the single most important idea for you?
   _____
   _____

3. What surprised you the most?
   _____
   _____

4. What did you disagree with or object to?
   _____
   _____

5. What did you most agree with?
   _____
   _____

6. What idea excited you the most?
   _____
   _____

7. Bob says that it's vitally important to study. What would you most like to study?
   _____
   _____

8. What is your reaction to this statement: personal development is a never-ending process?
   _____
   _____

9. Cybernetics is a central concept in this chapter. Write down a definition of *cybernetics* as you understand it.
   _____
   _____

10. Bob also discusses *unconscious competence*. Describe what this is as you understand it.
    _____
    _____

Discipline

"Discipline is the ability to give yourself a command and follow it . . ." writes Bob. Write down ten areas in which you believe you are well disciplined.

1. _____
2. _____
3. _____

4. _____
5. _____
6. _____
7. _____
8. _____
9. _____
10. _____

Look at the above list and circle the quality that has been of greatest value to you.

Now write down ten areas in which you wish you were much more disciplined than you are.

1. _____
2. _____
3. _____
4. _____
5. _____
6. _____
7. _____
8. _____
9. _____
10. _____

Now go over the second list, and draw a circle around the area that would make the most difference in your life if you were more disciplined in it. Can you think of a way of improving? Write down some thoughts here.

_____
_____
_____

Study

Study is an important theme in this chapter. Write down ten areas you feel you have studied with some thoroughness. They can come from any arena of life, including academic, professional, sports, or hobbies.

1. _____
2. _____
3. _____
4. _____
5. _____
6. _____
7. _____
8. _____
9. _____
10. _____

Go through this list and draw a circle around the item in which you think you are most proficient.

Below list ten areas that you feel you don't know very well but would like to learn and study more about.

1. _____
2. _____
3. _____
4. _____
5. _____
6. _____
7. _____
8. _____
9. _____
10. _____

Now go through the second list and circle the item that would most benefit you if you studied it more. Then write down below three ways in which you could learn more about this subject.

1. _____
   _____
2. _____
   _____
3. _____
   _____

How determined are you to follow through on studying this subject? Rate your determination on a scale of 1 to 5, with 1 being "not at all determined" and 5 being "totally determined."

           1   2   3   4   5

Thinking from the State Desired

Bob also discusses thinking from the state desired. Write down your understanding of what he means by this. Refer back to the book if necessary.

_____
_____
_____
_____
_____
_____
_____
_____
_____

Thinking from the state desired uses imagination. You form a vivid mental picture of yourself as having already reached your objective.

Try thinking from the state desired for yourself. Begin by thinking of a cherished goal—ideally, the one you most cherish. Imagine what it would be like to have achieved that goal. What would you be doing? Where would you be living? What would your personal relationships be like? How much money would you have? Imagine all of these things with as many of the senses as possible: visualize scenes. Imagine what you would hear people saying about you. Most importantly, how would you feel inside?

Write down a description of what you imagine below. Try to include as much detail as possible.

Chapter Quiz

This quiz follows the format of those for the previous chapters. Here are ten statements from chapter 4. Again, rate them in terms of how much you understand and agree with them. If you both understand and agree with a statement very strongly, rate it at 5. If you completely disagree with or don't understand it, rate it at 1. Rate it at 2, 3, or 4 if you're somewhere in between.

1. Don't understand or strongly disagree
2. Understand a little but disagree somewhat
3. Neither agree nor disagree
4. Mostly understand and agree
5. Understand and strongly agree

____ 1. "Because people don't know how to write a new paradigm, they don't really understand the force that they're up against when they try to change their habits."

____ 2. "The enemy is the paradigm."

____ 3. "To be successful in disciplining themselves, people have to understand what they're working with. They have to understand what paradigms are and what they're doing with them."

____ 4. "The body is a delicate and plastic instrument, which responds readily to the thoughts by which it is impressed, and habits of thought will produce their own effects, good or bad, upon it."

____ 5. "Ignorance is the cause of doubt and worry."

____ 6. "Everything just *is*. Our thinking determines whether it's good or bad."

____ 7. "All the great breakthroughs have been totally illogical."

_____ 8. "We've got the potential to do anything that our imagination will show us."

_____ 9. "There's no such thing as miracles. Everything happens by law."

_____ 10. "If you really want to live up to your potential, set some goals that scare the daylights out of you."

_____ Total

Scoring

Now add up the sum of the numbers you've written down. Here is how to interpret your score.

10–20. You don't seem to be very sympathetic to the ideas in this chapter or may not understand them.

20–30. You are resistant to these ideas, but not completely.

30–40. You're somewhat open to these ideas.

40–50. You understand and are very receptive to these ideas.

If your score is under 40, you may have some difficulty either understanding or accepting the ideas in this chapter. You may want to reread it. If your score is over 40, you can go on to chapter 5 with confidence.

Central Points

Now write down three points in this chapter that are most important for you.

1. _____
   _____
   _____

2. _____
   _____
   _____

3. _____
   _____
   _____

Chapter Five

How Your Beliefs Affect Your Paradigm

Read chapter 5 in Bob's book. Take a moment to check in with yourself. When you have finished, answer the following questions. As always, feel free to write as much as you like—either in the space below or in your notebook.

1. How did you feel after reading the chapter? Happy? Sad? Excited? Frustrated?

   _____
   _____

2. What was the single most important idea for you?

   _____
   _____

3. What surprised you the most?

   _____
   _____

4. What did you disagree with or object to?

   _____
   _____

5. What did you most agree with?

   _____
   _____

6. What idea excited you the most?

   _____
   _____

7. This statement appears in this chapter: "Our belief system is based upon our evaluation of something. And frequently, if we reevaluate a situation, our belief about that situation will change."

   _____
   _____

   Restate this point in your own words. See if you can apply this insight to a situation in your own life, and describe it.

   _____
   _____
   _____
   _____

8. Write down your thoughts about this statement: "You can believe something on a conscious level while not believing it on a subconscious level." Can you find any instances of this in your own experience?

   _____
   _____

Your Beliefs: A Starting Point

Bob says that, "We believe many things because we heard them over and over as children. They become part of our belief system." Below, write down ten core beliefs that were implanted in you in your childhood. If possible, identify the person or entity responsible for imparting that belief in you.

1. _____
2. _____
3. _____
4. _____
5. _____
6. _____
7. _____
8. _____
9. _____
10. _____

Now go through your list of statements and write down:
1. The belief that has served you BEST in your life.

_____

_____

2. The belief that has served you WORST in your life.

_____

_____

Reevaluating Beliefs

"We have to keep reevaluating our beliefs," writes Bob. Write down ten beliefs you have that you believe need to be reevaluated, changed, or discarded. They may include some of the beliefs you wrote down on the previous page, but you can include others as well.

1. _____
2. _____
3. _____
4. _____
5. _____
6. _____
7. _____
8. _____
9. _____
10. _____

Circle the belief that you feel it is most important to reevaluate or change.

Conscious versus Subconscious Beliefs

Bob says that, "When people's beliefs aren't manifesting in their lives, it can be because their subconscious has not yet absorbed the new belief." Write down five areas in which you are not seeing the results you are looking for.

1. _____
2. _____
3. _____
4. _____
5. _____

Now for each area, write down a subconscious belief that may be undermining it.

1. _____
2. _____
3. _____
4. _____
5. _____

Manifesting New Beliefs

"You're dealing with an infinite power; there's no end to what you can do . . ." Bob says. He's talking about your own potential. Write down five things that you would like to have or accomplish if you had no limitations whatsoever.

1. _____
2. _____
3. _____
4. _____
5. _____

Now circle the goal that is most important to you.

Overcoming Distractions

"Unfortunately, we are distracted all the time . . ." writes Bob. Write down five of the most distracting things in your life, personal or professional.

1. _____
2. _____
3. _____
4. _____
5. _____

Circle the distraction that is causing you the most trouble. Write down three possible strategies for removing or overcoming it.

1. _____
2. _____
3. _____

Now choose the single most important of these approaches and decide to apply it, starting today. Revisit this page tomorrow and see how well you have succeeded. You may wish to do this daily until you feel that this distraction has been removed. You can make some notes about your observations below.

_____
_____
_____
_____

Problem Solving on Paper

Choose five figures, historical or current, that you most admire.

1. _____
2. _____
3. _____
4. _____
5. _____

Sit at a table with at least six seats. Take a problem and write it out as clearly as you can. After you've written it out, go back and eliminate as many words as you can without losing the idea.

Then sit at a different place at the table. Put yourself in the mind of figure 1 that you've chosen. Ask, "How would this individual look at this problem?" Try to get into that person's energy. How would they perceive this issue? How would they look at it?

After you've played with the question like that, you may sit at another place and ask, "How would figure 2 look at this?" Then sit at yet another place and ask, "How would figure 3 look at this?" Do the same with figures 4 and 5. Use the space below to write down the insights you are getting from each figure.

Figure 1 _____
_____
_____

Figure 2 _____
_____
_____

Figure 3 _____
_____
_____

Figure 4 _____
_____
_____

Figure 5 _____
_____
_____

Write down some thoughts about how your own perspective on this problem has changed as a result of this exercise.

_____
_____
_____
_____
_____
_____

Chapter Quiz

Here are ten statements from chapter 5. Again, rate them in terms of how much you understand and agree with them. If you both understand and agree with a statement very strongly, rate it at 5. If you completely disagree with or don't understand it, rate it at 1. Rate it at 2, 3, or 4 if you're somewhere in between.

    1 Don't understand or strongly disagree
    2 Understand a little but disagree somewhat
    3 Neither agree nor disagree
    4 Mostly understand and agree
    5 Understand well and strongly agree

____ 1. "Many of the beliefs that we operate with are absolutely ridiculous."

____ 2. "It's the repetition that alters what's going on inside of you. It's the repetition of hearing an idea that will change your belief system."

____ 3. "When you keep hearing the same thing over and over again, you're going to start to believe it."

____ 4. "Our belief system can change, and it is changing all the time. This change should involve upward growth, expansion, and fuller expression, because we're spiritual beings, and spirit always moves toward expansion and fuller expression."

____ 5. "The average individual knows very little about himself or herself."

____ 6. "We have been given intellectual qualities that no other form of life, so far as we know, have been blessed with: perception, will, reason, imagination, memory, and intuition. Each of these faculties can be developed to a tremendous degree."

____ 7. "The emotions are in the driver's seat, they cause us to move, but the intellect dictates what goes into the emotional mind."

____ 8. "Regardless of the intellectual or physical abuse you're subjected to, no one can cause you to think something you do not want to think."

____ 9. "Thought is omnipresent; so is spirit."

____ 10. "When you're thinking, you're working with an enormous power."

____ Total

Scoring

Now add up the sum of the numbers you've written down. Here is how to interpret your score.

10–20. You don't seem to be very sympathetic to the ideas in this chapter or may not understand them.

20–30. You are resistant to these ideas, but not completely.

30–40. You're somewhat open to these ideas.

40–50. You understand and are very receptive to these ideas.

If your score is under 40, you may have some difficulty either understanding or accepting the ideas in this chapter. You may want to reread it. If your score is over 40, you can go on to chapter 6 with confidence.

Central Points

Write down three points from this chapter that are most significant to you.

1. _____
   _____
   _____

2. _____
   _____
   _____

3. _____
   _____
   _____

Chapter Six

The Paradigm for Power Performance

Read chapter 6 in Bob's book. Take a moment to check in with yourself. When you have finished, answer the following questions. Feel free to write as much as you like—either in the space below or in your notebook.

1. How did you feel after reading the chapter? Happy? Sad? Excited? Frustrated?

2. What was the single most important idea for you?

3. What surprised you the most?

4. What did you disagree with or object to?

5. What did you most agree with?
   _____
   _____

6. What idea excited you the most?
   _____
   _____

7. Here is one suggestion from this chapter: right before you go to bed, ask, "Now that my dream is fulfilled, how do I feel?" Try this for at least one night and record your reactions below.
   _____
   _____

8. Record your responses to this statement: "Comfort is not a good place to be. If you're really comfortable with everything in your life, you're stuck, you're going sideways; you're not growing at all."
   _____
   _____

Decision, Visualization, Discipline

In this chapter, Bob writes, "There are three things that a person absolutely must lock into if they really want to set a higher goal and go after it. The first is *decision*. The second is understanding *visualization*, and the third is *discipline*."

In the previous workbook chapter on page 50, you were asked to specify one goal that is most important to you.

Write it down here.

_____

Write down whether you are now determined to achieve this goal. If you have another goal that is more important to you, write it down instead. If you are not determined to achieve any particular goal at this time, skip the rest of this section and go on to the next.

Decision. Write down a firm, clear, brief statement of your goal in the present tense—as if you already have it. For example, "I am earning $250,000 a year."

_____

_____

Visualization. Sit quietly and calm your breath and your mind. When you are quiet within, visualize what it would look and feel like to have achieved this goal. Make your picture as vivid, precise, and detailed as you can. Feel it as real. You can record some notes here.

_____

_____

_____

_____

Discipline. Decide on and describe three practical steps you can take today to move toward this goal.

1. _____
2. _____
3. _____

Three days after writing these steps down, review them. Rate your success at following them, on a scale of 1 to 5, with 1 being "not at all," and 5 being "completely."   1   2   3   4   5

Do the same thing a week later. Write down how successful you have been at following them, on a scale of 1 to 5, with 1 being "not at all," and 5 being "completely."   1   2   3   4   5

Write down the step that you have been *most* successful in taking.

_____

_____

Write down the step that you have been *least* successful in taking.

_____

_____

What discipline would you need to create in your life to make these steps more of a habit? Write your answers here.

_____

_____

Your Power Life Script

Bob describes a Power Life Script: In the present tense and in your own voice, you write out how you want to live—everything you want—in as much detail as you can. It's always in the present tense, and you're always being thankful for it: "I am so happy and grateful now that . . ." Take your mind to that place, and live there. You describe what you're thinking, what you're doing, and how you're living. Write down your script below, in as much detail as possible:

I am so happy and grateful now that:

_____

_____

_____

_____

_____

An Accountability Partner

In this chapter, we read, "When you make an irrevocable commitment, and you have an accountability partner, you're accountable to that person. Pick an accountability partner whom you respect and who you believe respects you. You say, 'This I will do,' and they hold you accountable for that. You don't want to let them down. You don't want to look bad in their eyes. The odds of you doing it have increased substantially."

Choose an accountability partner: someone you know well and trust implicitly. Write that person's name down here.

_____

Contact that person, discuss this process, and if the other person agrees, you both decide that you are going to hold each other accountable, ideally on a daily basis. Choose how you will keep in touch (phone, Zoom, text, email) and at what time. Write the details down here.

_____

_____

Now write down the specific goals that your partner is to hold you accountable for.

_____

_____

Since this is a mutual process, you will also be holding your partner accountable for certain tasks and actions. Write these down here.

_____

_____

One week after beginning this process, check in with your partner about how it's been going for both of you. Write down your observations below.

_____
_____

Write down any insights about ways to improve your performance and accountability—and your partner's.

_____
_____

Autosuggestion

Bob recommends using autosuggestion to reinforce your positive thoughts in your subconscious mind. Write down ten affirmations that embody your positive thoughts and aspirations, again in the first person.

Examples:

I am a wise, loving, gifted, and disciplined individual.
I succeed in everything I set my mind to do.
I see the good in everything.

1. _____
2. _____
3. _____
4. _____
5. _____
6. _____
7. _____
8. _____
9. _____
10. _____

Now take these affirmations and write them down in a place where you can have access to them at all times: an index card in your pocket, or notes in your smartphone's notepad feature. You can also write them on Post-Its and put them up in places where you will see them frequently: above your computer, on your refrigerator, and so on.

A week after starting this process, evaluate your progress. How successfully have you been in implanting these affirmations in your mind? What effect have they had on your mood? How could you improve the process so that you feel them with more certainty and conviction? Write down your observations here.

_____
_____
_____
_____
_____
_____
_____
_____
_____

A Three-Step Approach

Bob sets out a method used by his friend Michael Beckwith. He said when anything happens, there's a three-step approach to it:

1. "Look at it and say, 'It is what it is'; accept it. It's either going to control you, or you're going to control it."
2. "Harvest the good. There's good in everything. The more you look for, the more you'll find."
3. "Forgive all the rest. Forgive, let it go, completely abandon it."

Try to use this process on at least one thing each day that you find upsetting. Write down your results on a day-by-day basis for the first five days.

1. _____

2. _____

3. _____

4. _____

5. _____

What are your observations? Do you find this process useful enough to continue with it? Write down some comments here.

_____
_____
_____
_____
_____
_____
_____
_____

Procrastination

We learn in this chapter that in order to achieve our goals, it is essential to eliminate procrastination. Write down five areas where you are most prone to procrastinate. Be as specific as possible. For example, instead of writing "Chronic lateness," write, "Not making it to work on time."

1. _____
2. _____
3. _____
4. _____
5. _____

Now write down five steps you can take to eliminate these forms of procrastination (for example, getting up earlier in the morning).

1. _____
2. _____
3. _____
4. _____
5. _____

Act immediately to implement these steps. One week after beginning this process, review what you have written above and evaluate your success on a scale of 1 to 5, with 1 being completely unsuccessful and 5 being completely successful.   1   2   3   4   5

List some observations about your relative success and failure, along with further suggestions that may help you improve your results.

_____
_____
_____
_____

Chapter Quiz

Here are ten statements from chapter 6. As before, rate them in terms of how much you understand and agree with them. If you both understand and agree with a statement very strongly, rate it at 5. If you completely disagree with or don't understand it, rate it at 1. Rate it at 2, 3, or 4 if you're somewhere in between.

    1 Don't understand or strongly disagree
    2 Understand a little but disagree somewhat
    3 Neither agree nor disagree
    4 Mostly understand and agree
    5 Understand well and strongly agree

____ 1. "You've got to be raising the bar for yourself all the time."
____ 2. "Energy is flowing through us, and it's up to us to direct it in any way we want."
____ 3. "Decide what you want, and act as if you have it."
____ 4. "The ways and means to accomplish our goals are already here. We just have to get in touch with them."
____ 5. "Imagination is something that all wise people use to create the good."
____ 6. "All prayers are answered."
____ 7. "This great dream, the surging dynamic thing invisible to all the world, except to the person who holds it, is responsible for every great advance of mankind."
____ 8. "You've got to be aware of what you're not good at. It's OK not to be good at it."
____ 9. "Comfort is not a good place to be."
____ 10. "Everybody's disciplined. Some people are disciplined regarding the wrong things."
____ Total

Scoring

Now add up the sum of the numbers you've written down. Here is how to interpret your score.

10–20. You don't seem to be very sympathetic to the ideas in this chapter or may not understand them.

20–30. You are resistant to these ideas, but not completely.

30–40. You're somewhat open to these ideas.

40–50. You understand and are very receptive to these ideas.

If your score is under 40, you may have some difficulty either understanding or accepting the ideas in this chapter. You may want to reread it. If your score is over 40, you can go on to chapter 7 with confidence.

Central Points

Write down three points from this chapter that are most significant to you.

1. _____
   _____
   _____

2. _____
   _____
   _____

3. _____
   _____
   _____

Chapter Seven

The Lessons of Gratitude in Freedom

Read chapter 7 in Bob's book. Take a moment to check in with yourself. When you have finished, answer the following questions.

1. How did you feel after reading the chapter? Happy? Sad? Excited? Frustrated?
   _____
   _____

2. What was the single most important idea for you?
   _____
   _____

3. What surprised you the most?
   _____
   _____

4. What did you disagree with or object to?
   _____
   _____

5. What did you most agree with?
   _____
   _____

6. What idea excited you the most?
   _____
   _____

7. Write down your responses to this statement: "When you put yourself onto a frequency of love, love is all you can attract." Do you agree or disagree? Why or why not?
   _____
   _____

8. Write down your response to this statement: "Respect yourself enough to walk away from anything that no longer serves you, helps you to grow, or makes you happy." Do you agree or disagree? Why or why not?
   _____
   _____

A Gratitude Journal

Write down ten things you're grateful for.

1. _____
2. _____
3. _____
4. _____
5. _____
6. _____
7. _____
8. _____
9. _____
10. _____

Now think of three people that are bothering you. Write their names down below, and send them love.

1. _____
2. _____
3. _____

Now totally relax for five minutes, and ask for good energy for the rest of the day.

Use this space to record any observations about your feelings and responses to this exercise.

_____
_____

You may want to include this exercise as a regular part of your daily practice, say in the early morning.

Sending Love

A variant of the previous exercise: Write down the names of ten people to whom you want to send love. It would be most interesting if you include a mix of people you genuinely love and some that you dislike.

1. _____
2. _____
3. _____
4. _____
5. _____
6. _____
7. _____
8. _____
9. _____
10. _____

What does it mean to send people love? Think about this practice and write down some thoughts about how you actually do it. You may, for example, mentally send them rays of white light (or light of some other color). Of course there is no single right way, but a good criterion for its efficacy is how you feel while doing it and afterward. If you have good feelings—feelings of warmth, love, and security—you are probably doing it right. If the process makes you irritated or dissatisfied, consider other ways of sending love. Or look within and try to see the internal obstacles you may be facing. As we have already seen, they can be either conscious or unconscious.

Peeling Off the Mask

A quote from this chapter, used by Bob in his seminars: "Peel off the mask of illusion, unshackle the chains of expectation, release the ingrained patterns learned, give up the stories of the past, let go of the fear. It's never too late to be who you really are."

Sit quietly and let your mind come to rest. Now slowly reread the passage above. Close your eyes. Mentally peel the mask of falseness and phoniness off your face. When you are finished, make sure to relax your face fully.

Now think of the expectations that you feel most acutely—the ones that you feel are most limiting your freedom. Visualize letting them go. You may, for example, imagine them as sentences written on pieces of paper that you send to the wind.

You can do the same thing with your fears, ingrained patterns, or stories of the past.

One possible use of this exercise is to record this passage in your own voice and play it back to yourself in parts. You can, for example, play, "Release the ingrained patterns learned," stop the recording, and visualize releasing them in whatever images that come most naturally to you. And so on with the other parts of this process. Feel free to experiment with any variations that you find valuable.

Use the space below to record your comments and observations about this exercise.

_____
_____
_____
_____
_____
_____

A useful way of continuing this exercise on a daily basis: whenever you think of it, relax your face fully. Note your changes in mood and attitude.

Responsibilities

This chapter discusses the pressure of responsibilities, some of which are genuine, and some of which are not: we often feel responsible for things that have little or nothing to do with us. Use this exercise to sort out between them. First, write out five things you are genuinely responsible for (such as family or work duties).

1. _____
2. _____
3. _____
4. _____
5. _____

Now write down five things for which you feel responsible, although in fact you are not. Anything that causes or leads to feelings of guilt is likely to be a good choice.

1. _____
2. _____
3. _____
4. _____
5. _____

Now look at the two lists you have written above. Note the differences between them. How does each item make you feel? Record your thoughts here.

_____
_____
_____
_____
_____

Do you see the value in letting go of the things you are not responsible for? Write down your thoughts.

_____
_____
_____
_____
_____

Chapter Quiz

Here are ten statements from chapter 7. As before, rate them in terms of how much you understand and agree with them. If you both understand and agree with a statement very strongly, rate it at 5. If you completely disagree with or don't understand it, rate it at 1. Rate it at 2, 3, or 4 if you're somewhere in between.

1. Don't understand or strongly disagree
2. Understand a little and/or disagree somewhat
3. Neither agree nor disagree
4. Mostly understand and agree
5. Understand well and strongly agree

____ 1. "The entire process of mental adjustment and atonement can be summed up in one word, gratitude."

____ 2. "Gratitude is the attitude that hooks you up to your source of supply."

____ 3. "You've got to send love to those people who are bothering you: that puts you in a loving vibration. The benefit for you is enormous. Love everybody."

____ 4. "You are the only problem you will ever have, and you are the only solution."

____ 5. "You cannot escape from a prison if you don't know you're in one."

____ 6. "We're the only ones who can set ourselves free."

____ 7. "Freedom comes from understanding ourselves and our relationship with our God."

____ 8. "Anyone can create financial freedom in a relatively short period of time. To do that, they have to create a new paradigm. They should go to somebody who knows how to create financial freedom and then do exactly what that person tells them."

____ 9. "We shouldn't try to impose our own thoughts on other people."

____ 10. "It's up to us to recognize what beliefs we are operating with that are false and get rid of them."

____ Total

Scoring

Now add up the sum of the numbers you've written down. Here is how to interpret your score.

10–20. You don't seem to be very sympathetic to the ideas in this chapter or may not understand them.

20–30. You are resistant to these ideas, but not completely.

30–40. You're somewhat open to these ideas.

40–50. You understand and are very receptive to these ideas.

If your score is under 40, you may have some difficulty either understanding or accepting the ideas in this chapter. You may want to reread it. If your score is over 40, you can go on to chapter 8 with confidence.

Central Points

Write down three points from this chapter that are most significant to you.

1. _____
   _____
   _____

2. _____
   _____
   _____

3. _____
   _____
   _____

Chapter Eight

The Benefits of Changing Your Paradigm

Read chapter 8 in Bob's book. Take a moment to check in with yourself. When you have finished, answer the following questions. Feel free to write as much as you like—either in the space below or in your notebook.

1. How did you feel after reading the chapter? Happy? Sad? Excited? Frustrated?

2. What was the single most important idea for you?

3. What surprised you the most?

4. What did you disagree with or object to?

5. What did you most agree with?
   _____
   _____

6. What idea excited you the most?
   _____
   _____

7. How do you respond to these words of Bob's? "My perception of life kept me stuck where I was. I thought this was normal for me. It wasn't normal at all, but I accepted it because I really didn't think I could change it." Does this have any application to your life?
   _____
   _____

8. Another quote from the chapter: "There's a clear, unadulterated power that flows to and through us." Do you understand what this means? Do you have any experience of it? Write down some observations.
   _____
   _____

Benefits of Changing Your Paradigm

This chapter is about the benefits of changing your paradigm. Make a list of ten benefits that you will find particularly important or valuable if you change your paradigm.

1. _____
2. _____
3. _____
4. _____
5. _____
6. _____

7. _____
8. _____
9. _____
10. _____

Time Management

This chapter contains this quote from inspirational leader Earl Nightingale: "I've never mastered time management; nobody does. Time can't be managed. I merely manage activities. I merely write down at night what I'm going to do the next day. The next day I wake up, and I do those things. It's all decided."

Try this practice for yourself. At the end of your day, write down a list of tasks that you are going to do the next day:

1. _____
2. _____
3. _____
4. _____
5. _____
6. _____
7. _____
8. _____
9. _____
10. _____

Now circle the single most important task you have to carry out. It's often helpful to do that one first the next day. Sometimes, though, you may find that you are particularly dreading something (making a phone call, say), even if it's not the most important. You may want to do this first, which will give you a feeling of relief that will help you go on to the other tasks.

Delegating Tasks

The chapter emphasizes the importance of delegating: assigning tasks to someone else instead of doing them yourself. Make a list of five things that you are doing that you could delegate to someone else. For example, you may have an assistant at work who can perform some jobs that you are doing yourself.

You don't need to limit this list to the workplace: for example, you may find it easier and even more economical to hire someone to mow your lawn than to do it yourself. You may decide that two hours of rest on a weekend afternoon is far more valuable to you than the mowing cost.

1. _____
2. _____
3. _____
4. _____
5. _____

Logic and Illogic

In this chapter, Bob writes, "I'm not interested in whether something is logical or illogical. The question is, do you want it? Do you want to do it? Do you want it to happen? Then forget logic; just go do it." Write down five things that you want to happen—the more illogical, the better.

1. _____
2. _____
3. _____
4. _____
5. _____

Making More Money

Making more money is a major theme of this chapter. Write down how much money you are making per year right now.

_____

Now write down how much you would like to be making a year from now.

_____

How much would you like to be making five years from now?

_____

How much money would you like to be making ten years from now?

_____

Write down five steps that you can take immediately to increase your income.

1. _____
2. _____
3. _____
4. _____
5. _____

Look at this list a week after you have written it. How successful have you been at taking these steps? Rate your performance on a scale of 1 to 5, with 1 being "not at all" and 5 being "extremely successful."

    1   2   3   4   5

If you are not satisfied with your progress, write down one way in which you could improve it.

_____

Multiple Sources of Income

Bob emphasizes that the best way to make a lot of money is to have multiple sources of income. List your three main sources of income right now.

1. _____
2. _____
3. _____

Now list three new areas of income that you could develop within the next year.

1. _____
2. _____
3. _____

Circle the one that seems most important and feasible to you. Now write down three steps you can take to accomplish this goal.

1. _____
2. _____
3. _____

Chapter Quiz

Here are ten statements from chapter 8. As before, rate them in terms of how much you understand and agree with them. If you both understand and agree with a statement very strongly, rate it at 5. If you completely disagree with or don't understand it, rate it at 1. Rate it at 2, 3, or 4 if you're somewhere in between.

1 Don't understand or strongly disagree
2 Understand a little and/or disagree somewhat
3 Neither agree nor disagree
4 Mostly understand and agree
5 Understand well and strongly agree

____ 1. "Perception is a mental tool. It is to the mind what hearing or sight is to the body."

____ 2. "Everybody gets exactly the same amount of time, so it's what we do with our time that makes a difference."

____ 3. "With a sense of urgency, you get a lot done in a short time, in a calm, confident manner."

____ 4. "No one's more creative than anyone else. We are all creative; it's just that some utilize their creative abilities more."

____ 5. "If you're struggling, you're doing it wrong. If you're working in harmony with the law, it's going to be a free flow."

____ 6. "We've got awesome powers locked up within us that we're really not familiar with."

____ 7. "Money is earned not by work, but by providing a service. The more creative you are, the more service you can render."

____ 8. "Everything we could ever want is already here. We've got to get in harmony with it."

____ 9. "Don't talk about your health unless you're talking to a doctor."

____ 10. "Anyone who wants anything they haven't got should write down what they want in the present tense."

____ Total

Scoring

Now add up the sum of the numbers you've written down. Here is how to interpret your score.

10–20. You don't seem to be very sympathetic to the ideas in this chapter or may not understand them.

20–30. You are resistant to these ideas, but not completely.

30–40. You're somewhat open to these ideas.

40–50. You understand and are very receptive to these ideas.

If your score is under 40, you may have some difficulty either understanding or accepting the ideas in this chapter. You may want to reread it. If your score is over 40, you can go on to chapter 9 with confidence.

Central Points

Write down three points from this chapter that are most significant to you.

1. _____
   _____
   _____

2. _____
   _____
   _____

3. _____
   _____
   _____

Chapter Nine

Making Your Positive Paradigm a Habit for Life

Read chapter 9 in Bob's book. Take a moment to check in with yourself. When you have finished, answer the following questions.

1. How did you feel after reading the chapter? Happy? Sad? Excited? Frustrated?
   _____
   _____

2. What was the single most important idea for you?
   _____
   _____

3. What surprised you the most?
   _____
   _____

4. What did you disagree with or object to?
   _____
   _____

5. What did you most agree with?
   _____
   _____

6. What idea excited you the most?
   _____
   _____

7. In this chapter, Bob writes: "With both faith and fear, you're believing in something you can't see. If you've got a choice, it makes sense to choose faith." Write down your reflections on this point.
   _____
   _____

8. Bob writes: "Nothing is created or destroyed. Everything you require is already here. It's a matter of getting in harmony with it." Write down your reflections on this point.
   _____
   _____

Study

In this chapter, Bob stresses the importance of studying for success. Make a list of five things that you could study that could most improve your income.

1. _____
2. _____
3. _____
4. _____
5. _____

Now make a list of five things that you would like to study simply because you enjoy them.

1. _____
2. _____
3. _____

4. _____

5. _____

Compare your two lists. How do they relate to each other? Do they overlap? The workbook for chapter 4 had a similar exercise for study on page 39. Compare your two lists and write down some thoughts that occur to you along these lines.

Eight Principles for Living

Eight principles for living are set out in this chapter. They are listed below. First, rate on a scale of 1 to 5 your own level of commitment to following these principles. Next, write down your observations about your commitment and how to increase it if you choose. You may want to go back to Bob's book and reread the relevant sections to jog your memory.

1. Develop an awareness of your infinite potential.
   1   2   3   4   5
   _____

2. Act on what you want.
   1   2   3   4   5
   _____

3. Make a decision.
   1   2   3   4   5
   _____

4. Total commitment.
   1   2   3   4   5
   _____

5. Accountability.
   1   2   3   4   5
   _____

6. Focus.

    1   2   3   4   5

_____

7. Discipline.

    1   2   3   4   5

_____

8. Visioneering.

    1   2   3   4   5

_____

Reading in Partnership

Here is a recommendation from chapter 9: "I suggest that you commit to reading from this book every morning for thirty minutes for sixty days. I also recommend involving a partner in this project. Find a friend. If they don't have a copy of this book, buy one and give it to them. Write a little note in it. They will love you for it. Then say, 'I would like to study this book with you every day for thirty minutes. Make me accountable, and I'll hold you accountable. At the end of the thirty minutes, we'll check in and discuss what we've learned.'"

Find a person you can read this book with and who will make the same commitment to read from it for thirty minutes each day. Write down this person's name here.

_____

1. On the first day of your reading, check in with your partner as recommended. Make some notes here about your observations.

_____

2. Do the same on the second day. Write down your observations.

_____

3. Do the same on the third day.
   _____

4. Do the same on the fourth day.
   _____

5. Do the same on the fifth day.
   _____

6. Do the same on the sixth day.
   _____

Continue this process for the full sixty days. Write down your observations here. (Or, as always, you can also write them down in a notebook that you have dedicated to this purpose.)

Day 7   _____
Day 8   _____
Day 9   _____
Day 10 _____
Day 11 _____
Day 12 _____
Day 13 _____
Day 14 _____
Day 15 _____
Day 16 _____
Day 17 _____
Day 18 _____
Day 19 _____
Day 20 _____
Day 21 _____
Day 22 _____
Day 23 _____
Day 24 _____
Day 25 _____

Day 26 _____
Day 27 _____
Day 28 _____
Day 29 _____
Day 30 _____

On day 31, review your notes and discuss your observations with your partner. How do you plan to continue your learning? Write down your observations and commitments here.

_____
_____
_____
_____
_____
_____
_____
_____

Go through this same regimen for a full 60 days, making notes of your observations as you go.

Practicing Concentration

Bob writes: "You can develop your will by taking a candle in a holder and putting it opposite your favorite chair. When you're alone, light the candle, sit and stare at the flame, and keep staring at the flame until you become one with the flame. If your mind wanders, which it will, bring it back to the flame. Every time it wanders, bring it back; don't feel bad, just bring it back."

Try this practice. Begin with three minutes a day. Then add a minute each day until you reach ten minutes. Write down your observations from this practice:

Day 1 _____
_____
Day 2 _____
_____
Day 3 _____
_____
Day 4 _____
_____
Day 5 _____
_____
Day 6 _____
_____
Day 7 _____
_____
Day 8 _____
_____
Day 9 _____
_____
Day 10 _____
_____

Chapter Quiz

Here are ten statements from chapter 9. As before, rate them in terms of how much you understand and agree with them. If you both understand and agree with a statement very strongly, rate it at 5. If you completely disagree with or don't understand it, rate it at 1. Rate it at 2, 3, or 4 if you're somewhere in between.

1. Don't understand or strongly disagree
2. Understand a little and/or disagree somewhat
3. Neither agree nor disagree
4. Mostly understand and agree
5. Understand well and strongly agree

____ 1. "Knowledge is omnipresent. There's no need for a person to remain in ignorance."

____ 2. "The opposite of doubt and worry, on the positive frequency, is understanding."

____ 3. "You get the book, read it, and read it again and again."

____ 4. "Don't mix with people who haven't got big goals. Don't mix with people who want to talk about the news or rough times."

____ 5. "The only thing you can attract to you is that which is in harmony with you."

____ 6. "The imagination will take you anywhere."

____ 7. "Our spiritual DNA is perfect; it's in our heart, the heart of hearts, in universal intelligence."

____ 8. "When you're interested in something, you'll do it if it's convenient; when you're committed, you'll do it regardless."

____ 9. "When you can concentrate on one thing, you can concentrate on anything, because you've strengthened your will."

____ 10. "Order is heaven's first law."

____ Total

Scoring

Now add up the sum of the numbers you've written down. Here is how to interpret your score.

10–20. You don't seem to be very sympathetic to the ideas in this chapter or may not understand them.

20–30. You are resistant to these ideas, but not completely.

30–40. You're somewhat open to these ideas.

40–50. You understand and are very receptive to these ideas.

If your score is under 40, you may have some difficulty either understanding or accepting the ideas in this chapter. You may want to reread it. If your score is over 40, you can go on to chapter 10 with confidence.

Central Points

Write down three points from this chapter that are most significant to you.

1. _____

2. _____

3. _____

Chapter 10

Continuing On

*C*ongratulations! You have now studied and worked your way through *Change Your Paradigm, Change Your Life*. It's time for some summary. Below, write down five of the ideas in this book that have left the strongest impression on you.

1. _____
2. _____
3. _____
4. _____
5. _____

Now write down five of the practices recommended in this book that you find most useful.

1. _____
2. _____
3. _____
4. _____
5. _____

Rank these practices in order of importance to you (if you haven't already). Take the practice you have deemed most important and resolve to implement it on a daily basis. Write down how you will do this. Write it in the form of a commitment, for example, "I commit to reading from *Change Your Paradigm, Change Your Life* every day for thirty minutes." Or "I will practice the candle concentration every day for up to ten minutes."

_____

_____

Do this practice for seven days. Then add the second item on your list and commit yourself to implementing it in your life. Again, write down your commitment here and how you will carry it out.

_____

_____

Do this practice for seven days. Then add the third item on your list above and commit yourself to implementing it in your life. Write down your commitment here and how you will carry it out.

_____

_____

Do this practice for seven days. Then add the fourth item on your list above and commit yourself to implementing it in your life. Write down your commitment here and how you will carry it out.

_____

_____

Do this practice for seven days. Then add the fifth item on your list above and commit yourself to implementing it in your life. Write down your commitment here and how you will carry it out.

_____

_____

Some variation is possible in carrying out this practice. You can either *add* the new practice each week to the previous one, or in the second week, *replace* the new practice each week with the previous one. Obviously the second option is the easier one: choose between them according to an objective sense of your own commitment and energy.

Once you have gone through these practices, it's time to construct a daily regimen of your own that you will continue for the foreseeable future. Ideally, this regimen should include at least five of the practices recommended in this book. Write them down here, also stating how, when, and how long you will practice them.

1. _____

_____

_____

2. _____

_____

_____

3. _____

_____

_____

4. _____

_____

_____

5. _____

_____

_____

Finally . . .

Congratulations! You have not only worked your way through *Change Your Paradigm, Change Your Life* but have decided how you will implement its ideas and practices on a daily basis.

Since Bob recommends reading and rereading his book, you can also go back through this workbook, either in sequence or according to the passage you are reading for that day.

Note-taking is an important part of your improved paradigm. At this point (if you haven't already), you should consider getting and keeping a notebook that is exclusively devoted to your work with this book. This will give you ample space for all your thoughts and reflections. You can, if you like, make it into a daily journal as well.

Many blessings to you on your path!

www.ingramcontent.com/pod-product-compliance
Lightning Source LLC
Chambersburg PA
CBHW072216070526
44585CB00015B/1368